OVERCOMING
FRUSTRATION, ANGER, & EXHAUSTION

A CAREGIVER'S GUIDE

Dedication

To all the caregivers and their families who have faced frustration, anger, and exhaustion. You serve in one of the most underappreciated yet essential roles in society. I stand with you and commend your strength.

Keep caring, even when it's hard, because what you do truly impacts someone's life, even if they don't always recognize it.

Remember, *Caregivers Do Matter.*

Contents

As Caregiving Begins

When you begin your journey as a caregiver for an elderly relative, a child with special needs or other persons in need of home care, it can feel like the weight of the world is on your shoulders. You want to provide the best possible care, but you may not know what that entails. Before you jump into full-time caregiving, there are several things you should be aware of:

Evaluate your own health and well-being

Caregiving can be physically and emotionally taxing. It's important to make sure you are in good health before taking on this responsibility. This includes getting enough sleep, eating well, and exercising regularly. Don't be afraid to ask for help if you need it.

Understand your loved one's medical needs

It's crucial to have a thorough understanding of your loved one's medical needs before entering into full-time caregiving. This includes any medications they are taking, any medical conditions they may have, and any special dietary requirements. Make sure you have a clear plan in place for managing their medical care.

Create a schedule and routine

Creating a schedule and routine can help both you and your loved one adjust to the new caregiving arrangement. This can include setting specific times for meals, medications, and activities. It's important to be flexible and adaptable but having a basic routine in place can help provide structure and stability.

Educate yourself on caregiving best practices

There is a wealth of information available on best practices for caregiving. This may include techniques for managing common issues such as dementia or incontinence, tips for preventing falls, or advice on how to provide emotional support. Seek out resources such as support groups or online forums to connect with other caregivers and learn from their experiences.

Take care of yourself

Finally, it's important to remember to take care of yourself as well. This may mean taking breaks when you need them, being available for your own hobbies and interests, or seeking out professional counseling if necessary. Remember, you can't take care of someone else if you're not taking care of yourself.

By taking the time to understand your loved one's needs, creating a routine, educating yourself, and prioritizing self-care, you can provide the best possible care and ensure a positive experience for both you and your loved one.

"There are only four kinds of people in the world,

Those who have been *caregivers*.

Those who are currently *caregivers*.

Those who will be *caregivers*,

and those who will need a *caregiver*.

— *Rosalynn Carter*

CHAPTER 1 — FRUSTRATION

When will this ever end? Is there any light at the end of this long lonesome tunnel? Take comfort in knowing you are not alone. The "battle" of caregiving can be so intense at times you feel no one else could understand what you are going through. Most of the time you don't have energy enough to think about anything other than the person you are caring for. Taking care of a loved one, especially with diminished mental or physical capacities is at times overwhelming. With loving compassion, we continue to care even when the burden seems too much to bear.

The journey of caregiving may begin slowly, without notice. Your loved one becomes a little slower, displays a bit more forgetfulness, repeating stories, or questions more frequently, and is noticeably more irritable. They may even display irrational behavior or unexplained conversations with unseen guests. "Guess who I saw the other day at the ACME? Margaret!"

Of course, a whole story follows the beginning of yet another encounter that never happened. Her friend Margaret had passed away 40 years ago, not to mention our vivid storyteller has been home bound for several years now.

Caregiving could also come suddenly, without warning. You find yourself in a situation being the only person available to take care of an aging or ill loved one. Your life is upended by the massive task thrust upon you. Without training, support, or counseling you dive into the role, regardless, sinking or swimming. Hardly knowing which way to turn or who to contact for support, you muddle through the best way you can.

Frustration is just an event for some, but a lifestyle to those of us who are caregivers. For me it comes in waves, without prior notice. A simple dog barking outside, an unrecognized phone call, or the constant mumbling of our home bound bedridden house mate can begin the downward spiral towards complete frustration.

With no breaks in between the constant care, a person can suffer exhaustion. Well-meaning people will help. However, it takes time and energy to coordinate when help is most needed. Once exhaustion sets in, it becomes difficult to ask or receive help. You are running on fumes and need more than help – you need a break from the day to day, hour by hour constant care.

Caregiving experiences vary widely. While some take solace in the care provided by a close family member for their loved ones, for others, the journey is brief. In such cases, caregivers are spared from witnessing the gradual toll of chronic conditions on a person's physical, mental, and emotional well-being.

And so, caregivers, I salute you as you continue your journey of caregiving while learning on the job. I encourage you to accept the fact that you will experience frustration which may lead to anger on occasions. You are not alone.

Frustration in Caregiving

Frustration in full-time caregivers refers to the feelings of dissatisfaction, exasperation, and emotional strain experienced by individuals who manage providing continuous care and support to another person. Full-time caregivers often face significant challenges, including the physical and emotional demands of caregiving, the loss of personal time and freedom, financial burdens, and the potential for burnout.

As the aging population increases, there is a growing need for full-time caregivers. These caregivers handle providing long-term care to individuals who require help with their daily activities due to chronic illnesses or disabilities.

However, being a full-time caregiver can be overwhelming and often leads to frustration. If not addressed promptly, this frustration can become chronic and result in burnout. This book will discuss the causes, effects, signs, and strategies for overcoming frustration in full-time caregivers. It will also discuss how frustration often leads to anger along with many other emotions that affect the caregiver and the one being cared for.

"Caregivers DO Matter."

Angelic's Dilemma with Dementia

As Angelic embarked on the challenging journey of being a caregiver to her husband Mark, little did she know the emotional roller coaster that awaited her. The first signs of dementia in Mark marked the beginning of a long and arduous road ahead for Angie. Here's a poignant account of Angie's struggle as she navigated through the complexities of caring for a loved one with dementia.

Angie vividly recalls the day when she first noticed subtle changes in Mark's behavior. The forgotten keys, the misplaced items, and the confusion in his eyes were early indicators that something was amiss. As the diagnosis of dementia gradually unfolded,

Angie found herself thrust into the role of a caregiver, a role she never imagined she would assume.

The progression of Mark's dementia brought forth a myriad of challenges for Angie. The constant repetition of questions and requests became a daily occurrence. "Are you going to the store?" "Can you bring me a cup of coffee?" "What do we have good to eat?" These relentless queries echoed through their home, each repetition chipping away at Angie's patience and emotional well-being.

The sleepless nights became Angie's new normal as Mark's conversations with himself pierced through the silence of the night. The weight of exhaustion bore heavy on Angie's shoulders, affecting her ability to function during the day. The physical and emotional toll of sleep deprivation threatened to engulf Angie in a whirlpool of frustration and hopelessness.

Recognizing the importance of seeking support, Angie reached out to support groups and counseling services. Through shared experiences and coping strategies discussed with fellow caregivers, Angie found solace in knowing that she was not alone in her struggles. Connecting with others who understood her journey provided Angie with a sense of camaraderie and understanding.

The challenge of communicating with Mark, who often repeated the same questions without recollection, tested Angie's patience and empathy. "Mark, you just asked me that not ten minutes ago. Don't you remember?" Mark just stared motionlessly as if trying to recall the recent conversation. "No, I don't remember, I'm sorry I bothered you," he quietly responded. (Of course, he asked the same question a few minutes later.)

Developing strategies to redirect Mark's queries and engaging him in meaningful activities became Angie's daily endeavor. Through trial and error, Angie learned to navigate the maze of communication challenges that dementia presented.

The decision to move to separate bedrooms was a heart-wrenching choice for Angie. The need for uninterrupted sleep and personal space led Angie to take this step, albeit with a heavy heart. The physical separation from Mark in the nights brought a mix of relief and guilt, as Angie grappled with the emotional turmoil of balancing her needs with her caregiving responsibilities.

To cope with the emotional strain of caregiving, Angie turned to mindfulness practices, journaling, and seeking moments of respite throughout the day. Engaging in activities that brought her joy and relaxation became essential for keeping her emotional well-being amidst the chaos of caregiving.

Recognizing the importance of professional guidance, Angie sought advice from medical professionals and dementia care experts. Exploring innovative care options and tailored strategies for managing Mark's symptoms became instrumental in providing holistic care for her beloved husband.

The delicate balance between self-care and caregiving became Angie's priority. Understanding that her well-being was crucial in providing quality care to Mark, Angie dedicated time to nurturing her own needs and interests. Embracing self-compassion and setting boundaries became Angie's guiding principles in navigating the challenges of caregiving.

Maintaining open communication with Mark while setting clear boundaries became Angie's cornerstone in fostering a harmonious caregiver-patient relationship. The art of empathetic listening and confirming Mark's emotions helped Angie create a safe and supportive environment for both of them.

Guilt, like a shadow, loomed over Angie's every decision and action. The constant battle between fulfilling her caregiving duties and attending to her own needs left Angie entangled in a web of guilt and self-doubt. Addressing these emotions with empathy and self-compassion became Angie's means of untangling the knots of emotional burden.

The metamorphosis of Angie and Mark's relationship under the veil of dementia brought forth a new dynamic that needed adaptation and understanding. Navigating the shifts in roles and responsibilities, Angie embraced the evolving nature of their bond with resilience and grace.

As the journey with dementia progressed, Angie found herself contemplating end-of-life care options for Mark. Engaging in discussions about hospice care, palliative services, and advanced directives became essential in preparing for the inevitable transitions that lay ahead. Angie's unwavering commitment to ensuring Mark's comfort and dignity in his final stages exemplified her profound love and devotion as a caregiver.

In the depths of caregiving for a loved one with dementia, Angie found strength in vulnerability, resilience in adversity, and love in moments of chaos. Her unwavering dedication to caring for Mark amidst the challenges of dementia illuminated the profound bond that transcended memory and time.

Through her story, Angie epitomizes the essence of unconditional love and selfless devotion that defines the noble role of a caregiver.

Causes of Frustration in Caregivers

Heavy Workload: Full-time caregivers often must deal with the needs of their care receivers round the clock, which means they cannot take a break whenever they want. The heavy workload can become overwhelming, leading to frustration.

Personal Issues: Caregivers may have personal problems that can make it even harder for them to cope with caregiving. Personal problems, such as marital issues, financial struggles, or health concerns can lead to frustration and eventually burnout.

Financial Issues: Caregiving can be a full-time job, and any caregivers sacrifice their paid employment to provide care for their loved ones. This can lead to financial strain, especially when the caregiver is the sole provider for the family.

Lack of Support: Caregiving can become less overwhelming when the caregiver receives support from family, friends, or professional organizations. However, a lack of support can lead to frustration.

Lack of Knowledge: Some caregivers may not have the necessary skills and knowledge to provide proper care. This can make caregiving more demanding and frustrating.

Medical Conditions of the Care Receiver: The medical condition of the person receiving care can also contribute to frustration. Conditions such as dementia or Alzheimer's can lead to aggressive behavior, which can be challenging and frustrating for the caregiver.

Effects of Frustration in Caregivers
Frustration can lead to various negative effects, including:

- Emotional exhaustion
- Depression

- Anxiety
- Irritability
- Physical exhaustion
- Social isolation
- Health issues such as hypertension and heart disease

Signs of Frustration in Caregivers
Physical Signs

- Frequent headaches
- Fatigue
- Insomnia
- Loss of appetite
- Weight gain or loss
- Frequent colds or flu
- Digestive problems such as stomach ulcers

Emotional Signs

- Anger
- Anxiety
- Depression
- Guilt
- Hopelessness
- Irritability
- Mood swings
- Resentment

Behavioral Signs

- Neglecting personal hygiene
- Drug or alcohol abuse

- Social withdrawal
- Carelessness
- Aggressive behavior
- Poor judgment

Strategies for Overcoming Frustration in Caregivers

Self-Care

Caregivers should take care of their physical, emotional, and spiritual well-being. They can take breaks, practice relaxation techniques such as yoga or meditation, and keep healthy eating habits and exercise routines.

Seek Professional Help

Caregivers can seek professional help from healthcare professionals or support groups to manage their stress and frustration. Counselors or therapists can help caregivers cope with their emotions and build critical thinking skills.

Acceptance

Accepting that caregiving can be difficult, and frustrating can help caregivers develop a cheerful outlook towards caregiving. They should acknowledge that they cannot control everything and learn to let go of things they cannot change.

Critical Thinking Skills

Caregivers can develop critical thinking skills to learn how to prioritize tasks, set realistic goals, delegate responsibilities, and find solutions to problems.

Build Support Networks

Caregivers should build support networks of family, friends, professional organizations, and support groups. They can reach out to others for help when they need it.

Get Educated about Caregiving

Caregivers can enroll in caregiving education programs to obtain the necessary skills and knowledge to provide care effectively.

Ten Steps for Overcoming Frustration in Caregivers

Being a full-time caregiver comes with its own set of challenges. From managing daily tasks to ensuring the well-being of your loved ones, the role can be overwhelming at times. One common emotion that caregivers often face is frustration. In this article, we will explore ten steps that full-time caregivers can take to overcome frustration and navigate their caregiving journey with more ease.

1. Acknowledge Your Feelings:

It's essential to recognize and accept the feelings of frustration that arise. By acknowledging your emotions, you can work towards finding healthy ways to manage them effectively.

2. Seek Support from Others:

Don't hesitate to lean on friends, family, or support groups for emotional and practical help. Sharing your feelings with others can provide a sense of relief and connection.

3. Take Breaks and Prioritize Self-Care:

Remember that taking care of yourself is crucial in being able to care for others. Schedule regular breaks, engage in activities that bring you joy, and prioritize your physical and mental well-being.

4. Set up a Routine:

Creating a structured routine can help you stay organized and manage your time efficiently. Include time for caregiving tasks, self-care, and personal activities in your schedule.

5. Communicate with the Person You Are Caring For:

Open and honest communication with the person you are caring for is key to understanding their needs and building a supportive relationship. Listen actively and express your own feelings without judgment.

6. Use Available Resources:

Take advantage of caregiver support programs, online resources, and community services that can provide help and guidance tailored to your needs as a caregiver.

7. Practice Mindfulness & Stress Management Techniques:

Incorporate mindfulness practices, deep-breathing exercises, meditation, or yoga into your daily routine to help alleviate stress and keep a sense of calm amidst the challenges you face.

8. Find Moments of Joy and Gratitude:

Amidst the responsibilities of caregiving, remember to cherish the moments of joy and express gratitude for the positive aspects of your journey. Finding moments of happiness can uplift your spirits and reduce feelings of frustration.

9. Set Realistic Expectations:

Avoid putting excessive pressure on yourself and set realistic expectations. Understand that caregiving is a demanding role, and it's okay to seek help or take a step back when needed. Establish boundaries to protect your own well-being.

10. Implement the Steps:

By implementing these ten steps, full-time caregivers can navigate their caregiving journey with more resilience and overcome the challenges of frustration. Remember that seeking support, prioritizing self-care, and finding moments of joy are essential in supporting a healthy balance as a caregiver.

Results of Overcoming Frustration in Caregivers

Overcoming frustration leads to positive outcomes, including:

- Enhanced ability to provide quality care
- Improved physical, emotional, and spiritual well-being
- Better problem-solving and decision-making skills
- Better relationships with the care receiver
- Better coping skills
- Better work-life balance
- Reduced risk of burnout

Finally, frustration is a common emotion among caregivers, and if not addressed promptly, it can lead to burnout and other negative effects. Caregivers can overcome frustration by taking care of themselves, seeking professional help, accepting their limitations, developing critical thinking skills, building support networks, and getting educated about caregiving. Overcoming frustration can lead to better physical, emotional, and spiritual well-being, improved relationships with care receivers, better critical thinking skills, and better work-life balance.

Caring... In Spite Of

Kenisha, an African American caregiver had been in the caregiving profession for over a decade. She had encountered all types of clients, from the sweetest old ladies to the grumpiest old men. But one day, she was introduced to a new client, a 101-year-old white woman named Elizabeth, by her son Christopher.

As soon as Kenisha entered the room, Elizabeth started yelling and using racial slurs, including the n-word, telling her to leave and that she didn't want a "black person" in her house. Kenisha was taken aback and hurt by the woman's words, but she knew that this was not about her personally, but rather a reflection of the prejudices that Elizabeth had grown up with.

Despite the initial hostility, Kenisha resolved to be patient and compassionate with Elizabeth. She started by trying to find common ground with her, asking about her background and interests. As she listened to Elizabeth's stories about growing up in the deep south, being raised by parents who were racially intolerant, she began to realize that there was more to her than just her racist beliefs. Elizabeth spoke of her mother very fondly and told how she was taught to cook and sew, as well as how to be a "lady" in social settings.

Over time, Elizabeth's behavior towards Kenisha improved, and they even developed a close bond. Kenisha would bring her small gifts and treats, and they would spend hours chatting and laughing together. Christopher was amazed by the transformation and how much happier his mother was with Kenisha around.

One day, Christopher pulled Kenisha aside and asked her how she was able to deal with his mother's initial behavior. Kenisha replied, "To do this job, you need a little Jesus and a lot of patience." She explained that she had learned to not take things personally and to approach each client with empathy and understanding.

In the end, Kenisha's patience and compassion had paid off, and she had not only earned Elizabeth's trust and respect but also helped her to overcome some of her prejudices. It was a reminder that sometimes, the hardest people to love are the ones who need it the most. We should care in spite of.

Frequently Asked Questions: (FAQ's)

Why do I feel so frustrated and angry while caregiving?

It's common to feel frustrated when caring for someone who is difficult, especially when dealing with stress, exhaustion, and a lack of appreciation. Understanding these emotions can help you manage them better.

How do I prevent burnout while caring for someone who is difficult?

Take time for self-care, seek support from friends or professionals, and consider respite care options to give yourself a break. Burnout is a serious risk for caregivers.

What should I do if my loved one's behavior becomes abusive?

If your loved one becomes verbally, emotionally, or physically abusive, it's important to set clear boundaries and seek professional help. You may also need to consider alternative care options.

How can I balance caregiving with my personal life and responsibilities?

Creating a schedule, setting priorities, and accepting help can ease the burden. Caregiving is challenging, and finding a balance is crucial for your well-being.

Why do I feel resentment toward my loved one?

Resentment can build when caregiving responsibilities feel overwhelming or when you feel unappreciated. Acknowledging these feelings and seeking support can prevent them from escalating.

CHAPTER 2 — ANGER

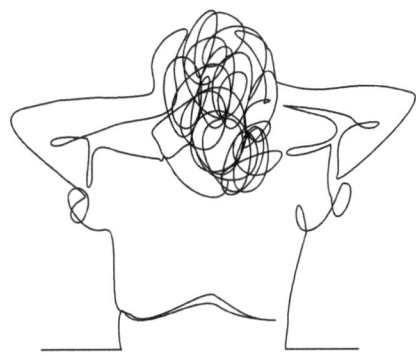

The feeling of being angry can vary for full-time caregivers depending on the situation and their individual experiences. However, some common definitions or descriptions of anger among full-time caregivers may include:

Anger is a strong emotion characterized by feelings of frustration, irritation, and annoyance in response to a perceived injustice, unfairness, or lack of control. Anger is a natural response to the stress and demands of caregiving, such as when dealing with difficult behaviors or challenging medical conditions of the care recipient. Anger is a complex emotion that can be triggered by a range of factors, including feelings of guilt, grief, or overwhelm, as well as external factors such as lack of support or resources.

Frustration can lead to anger

Overall, anger can be a normal and healthy response to certain situations, but it can also become problematic if it leads to aggressive or harmful behavior towards oneself or others. It is important for caregivers to recognize and manage their feelings of anger in a constructive and healthy way, with the help of support from others, self-care practices, and professional resources if needed.

As a full-time caregiver, it is not unusual to experience the perplexing and multifaceted emotion of anger. The task of caregiving is incredibly demanding and stressful, requiring intense physical and emotional energy. Consequently, feeling overwhelmed, frustrated, and experiencing moments of anger are common.

There are various reasons why anger can appear, such as feeling unsupported or unappreciated by others, believing that it is impossible to alter the situation, or sensing that your own needs and desires are subordinated to the role of caregiving.

Additionally, the person you are caring for could be the source of your anger, especially if they are in a situation where they cannot communicate or cooperate with you.

As a caregiver, it is important to acknowledge and recognize your anger instead of denying it. Not doing so can lead to a heightened level of emotional strife and further tension. Nevertheless, managing your anger in a healthy way is crucial, as inappropriate expressions of anger can have an adverse effect on both you and the person you are taking care of.

There are various ways available to control anger as a caregiver. Seeking help from family members, friends, or a professional counselor is one possibility. Engaging in stress reducing activities, e.g., meditation or exercise, setting practical expectations for yourself and others, and discovering ways to take a break and prioritize your own needs are all great techniques. Additionally, it is important to have open and honest communication with the person you are caring for and involve them in decision-making about their care.

Causes of Anger in Caregivers

Full-time caregiving can be overwhelming, and caregivers often take on more responsibilities than they can manage. This overload of responsibilities can lead to feelings of frustration and

anger. Lack of support is also a major cause of anger in full-time caregivers. Caregiving is often an isolating experience, and caregivers may feel unsupported and unappreciated. Additionally, emotional exhaustion, mental strain, and physical exhaustion are common causes of anger in full-time caregivers.

Thanksgiving in June

Millicent had always looked up to her Uncle Richard. He had been her hero since she was young, always there for her, providing guidance, and offering a helping hand. That's why when he needed her, she didn't hesitate to become his caregiver. She moved him into her small apartment, allowing him to bring his beloved cat, Joshua, and made sure he was well taken care of.

However, as time went on, Millicent realized that being a caregiver was not always easy, especially when someone you love is no longer the same person they used to be.

Initially, things went well, but as time passed, Richard's condition started deteriorating. He began to forget things and make mistakes. This came as a surprise to Millie, as he had always been regarded as highly intelligent and organized.

Now, her hero was failing, leaving her feeling bewildered and disappointed.

One day, in June, when Millicent came home from work, after staying late to make some overtime, she found that Richard had taken all the food out of the freezer and had cooked most of it. He had also put the hamburger in the oven without removing it from the Styrofoam container, creating a mess inside.

Millicent was livid; she yelled, flailed her arms, stomped around the kitchen, and dumped the poorly cooked food into the trash. "Why did you cook all the food, Uncle Richard? What were you trying to do?" she screamed at the top of her lungs. Richard stared blankly and asked why she was so angry. He was just trying to earn his keep and help her with Thanksgiving dinner. He didn't realize it was only June.

Millicent was at a loss for what to do. The man she had always admired for his intelligence was failing her. She had to remind herself that it wasn't Richard's fault—he was struggling with old age, and it was her job to take care of him.

"I'm sorry, Unc," Millicent said as she tried to compose herself. "I appreciate your efforts, but we can't eat this. It's not cooked properly."

Richard nodded, looking down at the floor.

"I know I'm not the same person I used to be, Millie," Richard said, his voice shaking. "I feel like a burden on you, and I don't like it."

Millicent's heart ached as she realized just how much her uncle was struggling. She took a deep breath and placed both of her hands on Richard's shoulders, looking into his eyes. "You're not a burden, Uncle Richard," said Millicent. "I love you, and I'm doing this because I want to. You took care of me when I was young, and now it's my turn to take care of you."

Richard looked up at Millicent, his eyes glistening with tears.

"You're a good woman, Millie," said Richard. "I'm lucky to have you in my life."

But for Millie, it wasn't about the food. It was about the frustration and fear that came with being a caregiver. She was overwhelmed with the responsibility of taking care of Richard and the added burden of having to teach him everything from scratch. It felt like the weight of the world was on her shoulders.

But this incident turned out to be a turning point for both. Millie realized that anger wasn't going to help and that she had to be patient and kind to him. She began explaining things in simple terms and taught him step-by-step how to cook. She even bought him a cookbook with easy-to-follow recipes, and they started cooking together.

Millicent was reminded that being a caregiver is not just about physically taking care of someone; it's also about taking care of them. It's a full-time job that requires patience, understanding, and compassion. It's not always easy, but it's worth it to help someone you love.

Millicent realized that her uncle may not be able to do things the way he used to, but that didn't mean he had lost his intelligence or worth. She decided to approach caregiving with empathy and positivity, and she and Richard grew closer than ever before.

Caring for a loved one can be difficult, but it's also an opportunity to show kindness and compassion. Sometimes, it's easy to forget that the person you're caring for may be struggling emotionally, and it's important to be patient and understanding. Millicent learned this lesson the hard way, but she grew closer to her uncle in the process. In the end, caregiving proved to be a rewarding and meaningful experience for both Millicent and Richard.

As a result, their relationship grew stronger, and Richard's condition improved. He started to remember things and take better care of himself. Millie was overjoyed to see the positive changes and appreciated the moments they spent together.

Being a caregiver is never easy. It requires patience, compassion, and a lot of sacrifice. But it's also a journey filled with lessons and redemption. As Millie discovered, taking care of someone you love means learning to understand their limitations, and most importantly, learning to love them unconditionally, even in the face of mistakes.

The experience taught her to be strong, be patient, and to never give up on someone she loves.

Effects of Anger on Caregivers

Anger can have serious effects on full-time caregivers. Caregivers who often experience anger are at risk for several health problems, such as high blood pressure, heart disease, and depression.

Additionally, their interpersonal relationships may suffer as well, as they tend to become irritable and withdraw from their loved ones.

Signs of Anger in Caregivers

It is important to recognize the signs of anger in full-time caregivers, as early intervention can prevent harmful consequences. Physical symptoms of anger may include headaches, muscle tension, and stomach problems. Emotional symptoms can manifest as feeling overwhelmed, irritable, or easily frustrated. Behavioral symptoms include yelling, arguing, or becoming physically aggressive.

Overcoming Anger in Caregivers

Caregivers who are experiencing anger should seek professional help, such as therapy or counseling. Joining support groups with other caregivers can also be beneficial. Practicing self-care is essential for caregivers, and taking time to engage in activities they enjoy can help reduce anger. Caregivers should not be afraid to ask for help from friends and family.

Results Over Time

Overcoming anger in full-time caregivers can have positive long-term effects. Caregivers who have learned to manage their anger report improved emotional and physical well-being, better quality of care for their loved ones, and strengthened interpersonal relationships. Seeking help and learning to cope with anger can lead to a more fulfilling caregiving experience.

How to Manage Anger

Handling anger in full-time caregivers requires managing expectations, setting boundaries, and practicing relaxation techniques. Caregivers should have realistic expectations of themselves and their loved ones and learn to ask for help when necessary. Setting boundaries for personal time and space can also help prevent feelings of anger. Relaxation techniques such as deep breathing, meditation, and yoga can help caregivers manage their emotions.

Finally, full-time caregivers may experience feelings of anger and frustration, but there are ways to overcome these emotions. Seeking professional help, practicing self-care, and managing expectations can all help caregivers manage anger and improve their quality of life.

The Boiling Point of Frustration

Pamela had always been a woman who took charge of her life. She was a successful business person who lived life on her own terms. However, when her mother Jean's dementia started progressing, Pamela knew that she had to move in with her mother to take care of her.

At first, Pamela thought she could manage everything. She believed she had the patience to deal with her mother's illogical decisions, losing things, and being uncooperative. However, as time passed, Pamela found herself becoming increasingly frustrated.

"Pam, where did you put my purse?" Jean asked one day, looking around the room.

"I didn't touch your purse, Mom. You left it somewhere," Pamela replied, trying to remain calm.

"I always keep it on the table next to my bed. You moved it," Jean insisted.

"I didn't move it, Mom. Please try to remember where you put it," Pamela said, her voice starting to rise.

"I don't know where it is. You're supposed to help me," Jean said, tears welling up in her eyes.

"I am helping you, Mom. But you must understand that I can't keep track of everything all the time," Pamela said, feeling her frustration boiling over.

Another time, Jean refused to take her medication, insisting that she didn't need it. Pamela tried to reason with her, but Jean was stubborn and uncooperative.

"Mom, you must take your medication. It's important for your health," Pamela said.

"I don't want to take it. It makes me feel sick," Jean replied.

"It's not supposed to make you feel sick, Mom. It's supposed to help you," Pamela said, her voice tinged with irritation. "I don't care. I'm not taking it," Jean said, crossing her arms.

Pamela felt like she was at her wit's end. Her frustration was affecting her mental and physical health. She started drinking more often, hoping to find some relief from the stress. But it only made things worse. She even started experimenting with cocaine, which was a dangerous path to go down.

Eventually, Pamela realized that she needed help. She couldn't do this alone. She reached out to support groups and found a caregiver who could help her take care of her mother. With some help, Pamela was able to take care of her mother and take care of herself too. She started eating healthy, going for walks, and started painting as a hobby.

It wasn't easy, but with some help, Pamela was able to find a balance between taking care of her mother and taking care of herself. She learned that self-care was just as important as caring for others, especially when you're a primary caregiver.

Ten Steps for Overcoming Anger

Taking care of loved ones as a full-time caregiver is a noble and rewarding responsibility, but it can also bring about feelings of anger and frustration. Dealing with these emotions is essential for keeping your well-being and providing the best care possible. Here are ten practical steps to help full-time caregivers overcome anger:

1. Acknowledge Your Feelings: It's okay to feel angry at times. Recognize and accept your emotions without judgment.

2. Practice Self-Care: Prioritize your own well-being by taking time for yourself, engaging in activities you enjoy, and seeking support from friends and family.

3. Communicate Effectively: Share your feelings with a trusted person or therapist. Open and honest communication can help release pent-up emotions.

4. Practice Mindfulness: Stay present in the moment and cultivate gratitude for the good things in your life. Mindfulness can help reduce stress and anger.

5. Set Boundaries: Learn to say no when necessary and set up clear boundaries to avoid burnout and resentment.

6. Seek Professional Help: If anger persists and affects your daily life, consider seeking professional counseling or therapy for support.

7. Practice Relaxation Techniques: Incorporate relaxation techniques such as deep breathing, meditation, or yoga into your daily routine to manage stress and anger.

8. Take Breaks: Allow yourself regular breaks from caregiving duties to recharge and rejuvenate. Taking time off is essential for your mental and emotional well-being.

9. Focus on Positive Moments: Celebrate small victories and positive moments in your caregiving journey. Focus on the joy and fulfillment that caregiving can bring.

10. Find a Support System: Connect with other caregivers through support groups or online forums. Sharing experiences with others who understand can provide comfort and strength.

By following these ten steps, full-time caregivers can effectively manage and overcome anger, leading to a healthier and more fulfilling caregiving experience.

Scriptures to Overcome Frustration and Anger

The journey for full-time caregivers can be both rewarding and challenging. Caregivers often face moments of frustration and emotional exhaustion while providing care to their loved ones. In times of difficulty, turning to scriptures can offer solace, strength, and guidance. Here are ten impacting scriptures that can help full-time caregivers navigate through moments of frustration and find peace in their caregiving journey.

1. Receiving Comfort: Even though I walk through the darkest valley, I will fear no evil, for you are with me; your rod and your staff, they comfort me. – *Psalm 23*

These words remind caregivers that they are not alone in their struggles. It brings a sense of comfort and reassurance that there is divine support in times of hardship.

2. Finding Strength: I can do all this through him who gives me strength. – *Philippians 4:13*

In moments of exhaustion and feeling overwhelmed, caregivers can find strength and courage in these words. It reaffirms their ability to face challenges with resilience.

3. Gaining Patience: Because you know that the testing of your faith produces perseverance. Let perseverance finish its work so that you may be mature and complete, not lacking anything. – *James 1:3-4*

This scripture encourages caregivers to have patience and endure difficulties, knowing that challenges can lead to personal growth and strength.

4. Having Hope: Be joyful in hope, patient in affliction, faithful in prayer. – *Romans 12:12*

When facing challenging situations, caregivers can hold onto hope and remain steadfast in their faith. This scripture emphasizes the power of hope in supporting resilience.

5. Compassion and Kindness: Clothe yourselves with compassion, kindness, humility, gentleness, and patience. –*Colossians 3:12*

Caregivers can reflect on this scripture to cultivate a spirit of compassion and kindness towards themselves and others, fostering a sense of empathy in caregiving.

6. Trust and Believe: Trust in the Lord with all your heart and lean not on your own understanding; in all your ways submit to him, and he will make your paths straight. –*Proverbs 3:5-6*

This scripture reminds caregivers to trust in a higher purpose and believe in divine guidance, especially during challenging times.

7. Inner Peace: Do not be anxious about anything, but in every situation, by prayer and petition, with thanksgiving, present your requests to God. And the peace of God, which transcends all understanding, will guard your hearts and your minds in Christ Jesus. *–Philippians 4:6-7*

Caregivers can find inner peace and solace by turning to this scripture, practicing gratitude, and seeking peace through prayer.

8. Getting Rest: Come to me, all you who are weary and burdened, and I will give you rest.

This scripture serves as a reminder for caregivers to prioritize self-care and seek rest when feeling overwhelmed, allowing them to recharge and renew their spirits. – Matthew 11:28

9. Encouragement and Comfort: Praise be to the God and Father of our Lord Jesus Christ, the Father of compassion and the God of all comfort, who comforts us in all our troubles, so that we can comfort those in any trouble with the comfort we ourselves receive from God. *–2 Corinthians 1:3-4*

Caregivers can draw strength from this scripture, knowing that they are recipients of divine comfort and can offer the same solace to others in need.

10. Practice Perseverance: Therefore, since we are surrounded by such a great cloud of witnesses, let us throw off everything that hinders and the sin that so easily entangles. And let us run with perseverance the race marked out for us, fixing our eyes on Jesus, the pioneer and perfecter of faith. *– Hebrews 12:1-2*

This scripture encourages caregivers to persevere in their caregiving journey, staying focused on their purpose and running the race with endurance and faith.

Incorporating these scriptures into daily life can offer full-time caregivers strength, hope, and resilience in their caregiving role, helping them navigate challenges with faith and perseverance.

In conclusion, being a full-time caregiver comes with its unique set of challenges, and navigating through frustration can be overwhelming. However, by turning to scriptures for guidance and strength, caregivers can find solace and renewed hope in their caregiving journey. Incorporating these scriptures into daily life can offer comfort, peace, and resilience, empowering caregivers to face challenges with faith and perseverance.

Overcoming Anger with The Word

Caregivers should never hesitate to seek support from friends, family, or professional counselors. Connecting with others who understand the challenges of caregiving can provide comfort and validation, helping to alleviate feelings of anger and isolation. Building a support network is essential for caregivers to navigate their journey with strength and resilience.

Here are ten impactful scriptures that can help caregivers navigate through moments of anger and find calming solutions in their caregiving journey.

1. In your anger do not sin. Do not let the sun go down while you are still angry. – *Ephesians 4:26*

This highlights the importance of acknowledging and addressing anger promptly, emphasizing the need to resolve conflicts before allowing anger to escalate and negatively affect relationships and inner peace.

2. Whoever is patient has great understanding, but one who is quick-tempered displays folly. –*Proverbs 14:29*

This scripture encourages caregivers to practice patience and understanding, highlighting that impulsive reactions to anger can lead to regret and emphasizing the value of composure in difficult situations.

3. But now you must also rid yourselves of all such things as these: anger, rage, malice, slander, and filthy language from your lips. –*Colossians 3:8*

Caregivers are urged to release negative emotions like anger and embrace kindness and compassion, highlighting the need for a positive mindset.

4. My dear brothers and sisters, take note of this: Everyone should be quick to listen, slow to speak and slow to become angry, because human anger does not produce the righteousness that God wants. –*James 1:19-20*

Caregivers are encouraged to practice active listening and careful speech, noting that unchecked anger can obstruct righteous caregiving.

5. A gentle answer turns away wrath, but a harsh word stirs up anger. –*Proverbs 15:1*

This scripture underscores the power of gentle and wise communication in diffusing anger. It serves as a reminder for caregivers to respond with kindness and patience, even in tense moments.

6. Do not be quickly provoked in your spirit, for anger exists in the lap of fools. –*Ecclesiastes 7:9*

This scripture emphasizes the importance of gentle communication in diffusing anger, reminding caregivers to respond with kindness and patience in tense situations.

7. A person's wisdom yields patience; it is to one's glory to overlook an offense. –*Proverbs 19:11*

Highlighting the virtue of overlooking minor offenses, this scripture encourages caregivers to prioritize forgiveness and understanding over holding onto anger, promoting harmony and peace in caregiving relationships.

8. But the fruit of the Spirit is love, joy, peace, forbearance, kindness, goodness, faithfulness, gentleness and self-control. Against such things there is no law. – *Galatians 5:22-23*

By reminding caregivers of the fruits of the Spirit, including self-control and gentleness, this scripture encourages caregivers to draw upon these qualities to navigate and manage feelings of anger in a constructive and loving manner.

9. Refrain from anger and turn from wrath; do not fret—it leads only to evil. *–Psalm 37:8*

Caregivers are urged to refrain from anger and worry, as dwelling on negative emotions can lead to harmful outcomes. This scripture promotes a mindset focused on peace and trust in divine guidance.

10. Better a patient person than a warrior, one with self-control than one who takes a city. *–Proverbs 16:32*

Emphasizing the value of patience and self-control, this scripture contrasts impulsive actions driven by anger with the strength found in keeping composure. Caregivers are encouraged to show resilience and restraint in challenging moments.

These scriptures offer caregivers valuable insights and guidance on how to navigate and overcome feelings of anger, promoting emotional well-being, and fostering healthy relationships in their caregiving roles.

Benefits of Practicing Emotional Control through The Word

In a world where emotions can easily spiral out of control, it is essential to reflect on the profound wisdom shared in various scriptures. Let's examine how the teachings of different scriptures emphasize the importance of controlling our reactions and nurturing positive emotions.

Importance of Controlling Reactions

Understanding the implications of our words and actions and learning to respond with grace and understanding can transform our relationships and interactions.

Impact of Words on Emotions

Words have immense power to either soothe or provoke emotions. It is crucial to recognize the impact of our language on ourselves and those around us.

Real-Life Examples

John, a full-time caregiver for his elderly mother, found solace in daily meditation on relevant scriptures. Through this practice, he noticed a significant decrease in his anger episodes and a deeper sense of empathy towards his mother's needs. By applying these teachings, John was able to provide better care and keep his emotional balance.

These scriptures offer caregivers valuable insights and guidance on how to navigate and overcome feelings of anger, promoting emotional well-being, and fostering healthy relationships in their caregiving roles.

Finally, in the journey of caregiving, it is natural to experience moments of anger and frustration. However, by turning to scriptural guidance, practicing self-care, and seeking support, caregivers can navigate these emotions with grace and compassion. Remember that you are not alone in your challenges, and by leaning on faith and community, you can overcome anger and find peace in your caregiving role.

Frequently Asked Questions:

Can anger in full-time caregivers harm the care recipient?

Anger can negatively impact the care recipient's well-being and can increase the risk of burnout for caregivers.

Can therapy or counseling really help caregivers overcome anger?

Yes, therapy or counseling can be a valuable tool for caregivers who are struggling with anger and other emotions.

Is it normal to feel angry as a full-time caregiver?

It is normal to experience a range of emotions as a caregiver, including anger. Seeking help and support can help manage these emotions.

How do I cope with guilt when I feel angry at my loved one?

Guilt is a natural response, but it's important to remind yourself that your feelings are valid. Finding healthy outlets for your frustration can help, such as talking to a therapist or joining a support group.

What can I do when my loved one refuses to cooperate?

Try to remain calm and patient. Communicating clearly, setting boundaries, and working with a healthcare professional to develop strategies can help manage non-cooperative behaviors.

Is it okay to ask for help or take a break from caregiving?

Yes, asking for help is not a sign of failure. It's important to recognize your limits and reach out to others for assistance, whether from family, friends, or professional services.

Why do I feel resentment toward my loved one?

Resentment can build when caregiving responsibilities feel overwhelming or when you feel unappreciated. Acknowledging these feelings and seeking support can prevent them from escalating.

CHAPTER 3 — EXHAUSTION

Caregiver exhaustion, also known as burnout, is a state of physical, emotional and mental exhaustion. It may be accompanied by a change in attitude, from positive and caring to negative and unconcerned. Burnout can occur when caregivers do not receive the necessary help or when they attempt to do more than they are capable of both physically and financially.

Many caregivers also feel guilty if they spend time on themselves rather than on their ill or elderly loved ones. Caregivers who experience "burn out" may suffer from fatigue, stress, anxiety and depression.

Exhaustion is a common experience among full-time caregivers and can have significant negative effects on both the caregiver and the person receiving care. Caregiver exhaustion can lead to physical, emotional, and psychological distress and has long-term implications for the wellbeing of the caregiver. Therefore, it's crucial to understand the causes, signs, and methods of overcoming exhaustion to ensure adequate care for both the caregiver and the person they are caring for.

Causes of exhaustion in caregivers may include:

Over commitment: Many full-time caregivers take on too much responsibility, leading to a sense of being overwhelmed or overburdened.

Lack of Support: Caregiving in isolation can lead to feelings of loneliness and frustration.

Financial Strain: The financial burden of caregiving can place significant stress on caregivers and contribute to exhaustion.

Loss of Identity: Caregiving can often consume a person's identity, leading to a loss of self and exacerbating feelings of exhaustion.

The effects of exhaustion on caregivers can be serious and can include:

Physical Health Problems: Caregivers who suffer from exhaustion may experience physical symptoms such as headaches, muscle tension, and an increased susceptibility to illness.

Emotional Distress: Exhaustion can lead to emotional difficulties such as depression, anxiety, anger, and irritability.

Relationship Strain: Caregiver exhaustion can strain the caregiver's relationships with the person they are caring for, family members, and friends.

Some signs that a caregiver may be experiencing exhaustion include:

- Chronic fatigue
- Increased irritability or mood swings

- Difficulty concentrating or making decisions
- Neglecting one's own health and well-being
- Social withdrawal and isolation
- Increased use of drugs or alcohol
- Decreased interest in hobbies or activities

Overcoming exhaustion requires a multi-faceted approach, including:

- Seeking and accepting help from others
- Taking regular breaks and time for self-care
- Seeking counseling or support groups
- Prioritizing healthy habits such as exercise, nutrition, and sleep
- Finding ways to reduce stress and increase relaxation
- Engaging in activities that bring joy and fulfillment
- Setting realistic expectations and boundaries

The results of overcoming exhaustion can be significant, including:

- Improved physical and emotional health
- Increased energy and motivation
- Greater sense of purpose and fulfillment
- Improved relationships with loved ones
- Increased ability to provide quality care to the person being cared for

The Tired Twin

Barbara had always been close to her twin sister Brenda. They had been inseparable since childhood and had shared everything. So, when Brenda suffered a heart attack and stroke, Barbara knew that she had to step up and take care of her sister.

Being the primary caregiver wasn't easy for Brenda She needed a lot of hands-on care, and being fairly overweight with diabetes meant that she required a special diet. Barbara was constantly worried about not following doctors' orders and adding more stress to her already overworked schedule.

One day, while assisting Brenda with her physical therapy exercises, Barbara couldn't help expressing her concerns. "Brenda, I'm really worried that I'm not doing enough to take care of you. I feel like I'm not following the doctor's orders and it's adding more stress to my already busy schedule."

Brenda looked up at Barbara with a worried expression on her face. "I know it's hard, Barbara. But

you're doing the best you can.
I appreciate everything you're doing for me," she said.

Barbara let out a deep sigh and sat down next to Brenda. "I just wish there was a better solution. I'm exhausted, and I don't know how much longer I can keep this up."

Brenda thought for a moment before speaking. "What if we hired a professional caregiver? Someone who could help you with my care and take some of the burden off your shoulders?"

Barbara's eyes lit up at the suggestion. "That's a great idea! I don't know why I didn't think of it before. It would definitely make things easier for both of us."

With that, Brenda and Barbara decided to look into hiring a professional caregiver. They found someone who was experienced in caring for patients with similar conditions as Brenda and who could provide the extra help that Barbara needed.

The new caregiver quickly became a part of the family, and Barbara finally had the time to take care of herself and her own needs. Brenda's health improved, and Barbara's stress levels decreased significantly.

In the end, Barbara realized that being a caregiver didn't mean she had to do everything alone. Sometimes, the best solution was to reach out for help and find the support she needed to take care of her loved ones while also taking care of herself.

Ten Steps for Overcoming Exhaustion in Caregivers

Being a full-time caregiver can be physically, emotionally, and mentally exhausting. Here are 10 steps to help caregivers overcome exhaustion:

1. Acknowledge Your Feelings: Recognize and accept that it's normal to feel overwhelmed and exhausted as a caregiver. Acknowledge your feelings and understand that it's okay to ask for help.

2. Prioritize Self-Care: Take care of yourself first so you can better care for others. Be available for self-care activities such as exercise, meditation, hobbies, or spending time with friends and family.

3. Seek Support: Don't be afraid to ask for help from family, friends, or support groups. You can also consider hiring a professional caregiver or utilizing respite care services to give yourself a break.

4. Set Realistic Expectations: Understand your limitations and set realistic expectations for yourself. It's okay to say no to additional responsibilities and prioritize tasks based on importance.

5. Practice Time Management: Organize your daily tasks and responsibilities by creating a schedule or to-do list. This can help you manage your time effectively and reduce feelings of overwhelm.

6. Maintain a Healthy Lifestyle: Eat nutritious meals, get regular exercise, and ensure you get enough sleep. Taking care of your physical health can improve your overall well-being and energy levels.

7. Stay Connected: Stay connected with friends, family, or a support group to prevent feelings of isolation. Talking to others who understand your situation can provide emotional support and help you feel less alone.

8. Take Breaks: Make sure to take short breaks throughout the day to rest and recharge. Even a few minutes of relaxation can help reduce stress and prevent burnout.

9. Practice Mindfulness: Engage in mindfulness activities such as deep breathing, meditation, or yoga to help reduce stress and promote relaxation. Mindfulness can help you stay present and focused on the tasks at hand.

10. Seek Professional Help: If you're feeling overwhelmed or experiencing symptoms of depression or anxiety, consider seeking help from a mental health professional. Therapy or counseling can provide you with additional support and coping strategies.

Remember, taking care of yourself is essential in order to provide the best care for others. Prioritizing self-care and seeking support when needed can help you overcome exhaustion and continue to be a compassionate and effective caregiver.

Scriptures to Overcome Exhaustion

Here are ten scriptures that can serve as spiritual resources to help overcome exhaustion:

1. "Come to me, all you who are weary and burdened, and I will give you rest. Take my yoke upon you and learn from me, for I am gentle and humble in heart, and you will find rest for your souls. For my yoke is easy and my burden is light." *–Matthew 11:28-30*

2. "But those who hope in the Lord will renew their strength. They will soar on wings like eagles; they will run and not grow weary; they will walk and not be faint." *–Isaiah 40:31*

3. "The Lord is my shepherd; I shall not want. He makes me lie down in green pastures. He leads me beside still waters. He restores my soul. He leads me in paths of righteousness for his name's sake." *–Psalm 23:1-3*

4. "I can do all things through Christ who strengthens me." *–Philippians 4:13*

5. "And let us not grow weary of doing good, for in due season we will reap, if we do not give up." *–Galatians 6:9*

6. "God is our refuge and strength, an ever-present help in trouble." *–Psalm 46:1*

7. "Therefore we do not lose heart. Though outwardly we are wasting away, yet inwardly we are being renewed day by day. For our light and momentary troubles are achieving for us an eternal glory that far outweighs them all. So, we fix our eyes not on what is seen, but on what is unseen, since what is seen is temporary, but what is unseen is eternal." *–2 Corinthians 4:16-18*

8. "So do not fear, for I am with you; do not be dismayed, for I am your God. I will strengthen you and help you; I will uphold you with my righteous right hand." *–Isaiah 41:10*

9. "Whatever you do, work at it with all your heart, as working for the Lord, not for human masters, since you know that you will receive an inheritance from the Lord as a reward. It is the Lord Christ you are serving." *–Colossians 3:23-24*

10. "Therefore, since we are surrounded by such a great cloud of witnesses, let us throw off everything that hinders and the sin that so easily entangles.

And let us run with perseverance the race marked out for us, fixing our eyes on Jesus, the pioneer and perfecter of faith." *–Hebrews 12:1-2*

These scriptures can provide comfort, strength, and encouragement to those who are feeling exhausted and in need of spiritual renewal.

Exhaustion can lead to feelings of hopelessness

Hopelessness is the feeling that nothing can be done to improve a situation. It is a common feeling among full-time caregivers who are caring for their loved ones, but the demands of caregiving are too overwhelming. The word 'hopeless' can be attributed to caregivers as they often have few breaks and little time for self-care. Full-time caregiving can quickly become a 24/7 job, leaving little hope for relief. Without proper support caregivers can find themselves struggling to see the light at the end of the tunnel.

Hopelessness can lead to despair, depression, and burnout and may affect the quality of care they provide. Knowing the signs of hopelessness is crucial in getting the right care and support.

Being a full-time caregiver can be an overwhelming job. The person in this position is responsible for a multitude of tasks including administering medication, coordinating doctor's appointments, handling finances, assisting with bathing and grooming, and ensuring their loved one is safe and well-cared for. All of these duties are challenging and can lead to feelings of hopelessness in caregivers.

One of the most common issues that full-time caregivers face is hopelessness, which can manifest itself in many ways. In this article, we will explore the difference between burnout and hopelessness in caregivers, discuss how support groups can help alleviate feelings of hopelessness, and examine the relationship between hopelessness and stress.

What is the difference between burnout and hopelessness?

Caregiver burnout is a state of physical, emotional, and mental exhaustion that can occur when a person is responsible for the continuous care of a loved one. This condition can lead to fatigue, sleep deprivation, and a sense of detachment from the outside world. Burnout can be severe but is generally temporary and can be treated through a combination of rest, support, and self-care.

On the other hand, caregiver hopelessness is an overwhelming feeling of despair or a loss of self-efficacy. Unlike burnout, hopelessness can extend beyond caregiving responsibilities and can harm a caregiver's general quality of life. Hopelessness can induce feelings of worthlessness and enhance existing mental health disorders like depression and anxiety.

How can caregiving support groups help with feelings of hopelessness?

Caregiving support groups are an effective way to work with fellow caregivers and healthcare professionals to provide essential care for their loved ones. In these groups, caregivers can share their experiences, ask questions, and learn from other caregivers. Members can also receive emotional, educational, and social support and be a foundation of hope for one another.

Notably, caregivers often feel lonely or isolated, which adds to their mental load. Support groups are an excellent place to find understanding individuals who are facing similar challenges.

Therefore, joining a support group can be a powerful tool in combating caregiver hopelessness.

Can hopelessness lead to caregiving-related stress?

Yes, hopelessness is directly related to caregiving-related stress. As discussed earlier, caregiver hopelessness can significantly affect a caregiver's emotional well-being, leading to increased stress and anxiety. Hopelessness can make it harder to manage decision-making, amplifying feelings of stress and contributing to physical symptoms like fatigue, digestive problems, sleep disturbances, and headaches. Reevaluating daily caregiving routines, seeking support, and practicing self-care activities are essential steps towards managing caregiver stress.

It's Hopeless

Angel's heart sank as she received the news from her mom's doctor. Her mom, Maria, had been diagnosed with a chronic illness, but the doctors weren't sure what it was. Angel tried to hide her despair, but it was difficult as she had a huge meeting coming up at work. Being an executive in a major center city company in downtown Chicago came with its own stress, but now, with her mom's condition added to the mix, it seemed impossible to manage.

Maria doesn't speak English, and Angel found it hard to juggle her mom's situation with the upcoming meeting, making her feel emotionally drained, despairing, and anxious. These feelings which started to show up physically as headaches, fatigue, and stomach issues.

Angel's work was her passion, but being an only child to her mom, she couldn't ignore the new demands placed on her life. Angel felt the weight of the responsibility, but also the helplessness she faced due to the language barrier. To add to her worries, Maria's condition wasn't improving, and she was missing work. Angel felt as hopeless as her situation.

Angel had regular conversations with her good friend Gabriele, who worked in the same company, and was the only person at her workplace who knew about her mom's condition. Gabriele's empathetic personality made her the perfect person for Angel to confide in. She suggested taking time off work, but Angel felt conflicted and worried if her absence might negatively impact her job. Gabriele understood and offered to be there for her in whatever way Angel needed her. They both left for lunch, and Gabriele helped Angel confront her feelings about not being able to manage both situations at once.

Angel was hesitant to inform her boss, but the situation had reaching a breaking point. She could no longer juggle her mom's illness and her work. Finally, Angel mustered the courage to have a conversation with her boss about her situation. Angel explained the language barrier issue to her boss and how it affected her ability to care for her mom while dealing with a demanding job. Her boss listened, attentively, and Angel felt grateful for their support. In fact, her boss not only empathized with her situation but also expressed admiration for how Angel had been managing her work thus far. For the first time, Angel felt like the weight on her shoulders had been lifted.

The language barrier came into play when Angel took her mom to the doctor's office. The doctor spoke English, but her mom didn't understand the medical jargon, and it was frustrating for both Angel and Maria. "What does that mean?" was a common question that Maria asked Angel, and Angel would explain what the doctor meant in Spanish. However, Angel still didn't understand fully what was happening with her mom.

"Is there any progress?" Angel would ask, to which the doctor would say, "We are still waiting for further tests; we will keep you informed." These conversations were frustrating because there was no definitive answer which made Angel more and more depressed.

Angel felt that when words fail, emotion speaks louder. The fear of the unknown was the worst feeling, but caring for her mom and keeping up with her job was even more overwhelming. Angel tried to manage both the best she could, but sometimes it seemed that there weren't enough hours in a day. Sometimes, Angel would force a smile to cover up her unease in front of her mom when she felt like breaking down.

Sometimes, all it takes is one act of kindness to improve your day. At work, Angel received a package that was dropped off at her workplace desk. It was a gourmet basket with a note from Gabriele that read, "Thinking of you! Hope this brightens your day!" The gesture made a big difference to Angel, and she felt incredibly grateful for the support she received from her friend, even on such a small scale.

Angel recognized that her mother's medical condition wasn't going to be easy and that it would continue to affect her work life. She needed to find ways to cope with the added stress on both fronts. Angel also realized that sharing her experience with those closest to her made a big difference.

By communicating with her boss, friend, and doctor, Angel was able to manage her work and mom's care a lot more effectively. This wasn't something she could manage on her own, and the support she received made a difference. Angel still had to juggle her time effectively, but knowing that her support system had her back felt empowering.

Being an executive at a major center city company in downtown Chicago came with its own set of demands. Adding Maria's illness to the mix was a significant challenge for Angel, who took on the role of caregiver for her mom. But through communication and support, Angel was able to balance both situations and move forward in her job and her life.

Angel's experience is one that is recognizable to many and emphasizes that it's OK to ask for help when needed. By confiding in those closest to her, Angel was able to gain the support she needed, allowing her to be the caregiver her mom needed and the executive her job required.

What are the effects of hopelessness?

The effects of hopelessness can be damaging, and it's important to seek help before it becomes too overwhelming. Hopelessness can lead to depression, health problems, and strained relationships with loved ones. Additionally, it can affect the quality of care the caregiver provides, leading to neglect of their loved one's needs.

What can caregivers do to prevent or alleviate hopelessness?

There are various techniques that can be helpful, including exercise, meditation, or talking to a therapist. Caregivers should also seek out support systems where they can connect with other caregivers, as this can be an excellent way to manage stress and gain helpful advice.

Staying positive is another important factor in preventing hopelessness. Finding joy in the small moments can make a huge difference in a caregiver's outlook. Caregivers can also seek out activities that bring them pleasure and provide an escape from caregiving responsibilities.

Finally, understanding the needs of caregivers is crucial. Caregivers need support and understanding from their loved ones, and it's important to recognize that caregiving is a job that requires immense amounts of patience and dedication. By recognizing these needs and providing support, caregivers can feel motivated to continue providing care in the best way possible.

As a caregiver, experiencing hopelessness can be overwhelming. Symptoms like stress, anxiety, and depression can impact one's quality of life and overall health. While hopelessness is common among caregivers, it is essential to recognize the signs and practice self-care, join a support group or seek professional help to overcome it. As discussed throughout this topic, there are various ways to address hopelessness, including sup-port groups, and therapeutic exercises. Therefore, caregivers must feel empowered to prioritize their mental and emotional well-being concerning their caregiving responsibilities.

In conclusion, hopelessness is a common feeling among full-time caregivers, and it's important to address this issue by seeking out support, finding appropriate coping mechanisms, and staying positive. Caregivers need to recognize that they are not alone in their struggles and should not be afraid to ask for help when needed.

Frequently Asked Questions:

What is caregiver burnout?

Caregiver burnout is a state of physical, emotional, and mental exhaustion that occurs when a caregiver is overwhelmed by the demands of caring for someone else.

How common is caregiver exhaustion?

Caregiver exhaustion is a common experience among full-time caregivers, with approximately 40-70% of caregivers reporting that they feel overwhelmed or overburdened.

What are some ways to prevent caregiver exhaustion?

Some ways to prevent caregiver exhaustion include taking regular breaks, seeking and accepting help from others, prioritizing self-care, and finding ways to reduce stress.

How can family members support a full-time caregiver?

Family members can support a full-time caregiver by offering help with caregiving tasks, providing emotional support, and ensuring the caregiver has regular breaks and time for self-care.

Can caregiver exhaustion lead to chronic illness?

Prolonged caregiver exhaustion can lead to the development of chronic health conditions such as heart disease, diabetes, and hypertension.

Is it possible to experience caregiver exhaustion and not know it?

Yes, many caregivers may not recognize that they are experiencing exhaustion or may believe that it's just a normal part of the caregiving experience.

Frequently Asked Questions:

What can caregivers do to prevent hopelessness?

Caregivers can take steps such as seeking support systems, taking breaks, and engaging in activities that bring them joy to prevent hopelessness.

What is the difference between burnout and hopelessness in caregivers?

Burnout is a state of physical, emotional, and mental exhaustion that can occur when a person is responsible for the continuous care of a loved one. In contrast, caregiver hopelessness is an overwhelming feeling of despair or loss of self-efficacy. It can extend beyond the specific caregiving responsibilities and harm a caregiver's overall quality of life.

How can caregiving support groups help with feelings of hopelessness?

Caregiving support groups are an effective way to work with fellow caregivers and healthcare professionals to provide crucial care for their loved ones. Joining a support group can help combat caregiver hopelessness by offering emotional, educational, and social support.

Can hopelessness lead to caregiving-related stress?

Yes, caregiver hopelessness directly correlates with caregiver-related stress, leading to increased stress and anxiety. Hopelessness can make it harder to manage caregiving duties, amplify stress, and contribute to physical symptoms like fatigue, digestive problems, sleep disturbances, and headaches.

How can hopelessness affect the caregiver's loved ones?

Hopelessness can lead to strained relationships with loved ones and neglect of their needs. It's important to address hopelessness to prevent further negative impacts on the caregiver's loved ones.

A CAREGIVER'S GUIDE TO OVERCOMING

CHAPTER 4 —

STRENGTH IN COMMUNITY
Building a Support Network for Caregivers

A support network for caregivers is a group of people who provide emotional, practical, and/or financial support to caregivers. This network may include family members, friends, neighbors, healthcare professionals, and support groups. Building a support network can help caregivers feel less isolated, reduce stress, and improve the quality of life for both the caregiver and the person receiving care.

Identifying Potential Sources of Support

The first step in building a support network as a caregiver is to identify potential sources of support. This can include family members, friends, neighbors, religious organizations, community centers, and support groups. It's important to reach out to people who you trust and who can provide the type of support you need, whether it's emotional, practical, or financial.

Joining a Support Group

One of the most effective ways to build a support network as a caregiver is to join a support group. Support groups allow caregivers to connect with others who are going through similar experiences, share their struggles and successes, and access valuable resources and information. Support groups can be found through local hospitals, community centers, and online forums.

Building Connections with Other Caregivers

Building connections with other caregivers is also an essential part of building a support network. Caregivers can attend local events, meet ups, and support group meetings to connect with others, share their experiences, and build relationships. It's important to listen to other caregivers and learn from their experiences, as well as share your own. This can help you feel less alone and more supported, as well as provide valuable insights and advice.

Building Relationships with Family and Friends

Caregiving for family can become a source for support as well as a source of distress. When relationships are strained or uncomfortable, caregiving for that person will take patience and wisdom to get through it. Keep in mind that you are not alone.

Caregivers can feel alone and abandoned at times. Learn to share your situation with those you trust will care. Building relationships with family and friends can be an important part of building a support network as a caregiver. It's important to be open and honest with loved ones about your experience as a caregiver, and to let them know what type of support you need. This can include help with household tasks, providing respite care, or simply being there to listen and provide emotional support.

Accessing Community Resources

Accessing community resources can also be an important part of building a support network as a caregiver. Local, state, and federal organizations often provide a range of programs and services designed to support caregivers, including respite care, counseling services, educational resources, and financial assistance. It's important to research these resources and take advantage of any that may be available to you.

Becoming an Advocate for Caregivers

Finally, caregivers can also become advocates for themselves and others by speaking out about their experiences and raising awareness about the challenges of caregiving. This can include participating in local and national caregiver organizations, speaking to lawmakers, and sharing their stories with the media. By advocating for themselves and others, caregivers can help create a more supportive and understanding community for all those who provide care for their loved ones.

Building a network of support is essential for caregivers, and finding strength in community is an excellent way to overcome the challenges of caregiving. By identifying potential sources of support, joining a support group, building connections with other caregivers, building relationships with family and friends, accessing community resources, and becoming an advocate for other caregivers, caregivers can build a strong and supportive network that can help them navigate the challenges of caregiving and maintain their own physical and emotional well-being.

Frequently Asked Questions:

What makes emotional support essential when building a support network for full-time caregivers?

Emotional support provides a listening ear and empathy to help caregivers reduce stress and burnout.

What benefits can in-person support groups offer to full-time caregivers compared to online support groups?

In-person support groups may provide more tangible emotional support since the group members meet face-to-face and can form deeper connections.

How can support groups for full-time caregivers help them to better handle stress?

Support groups offer a safe space for caregivers to share their experiences and receive advice on how to manage stress.

What strategies can a full-time caregiver utilize to maintain a strong support network?

Maintaining a strong network involves regular check-ins, updates, and expressions of gratitude to support group members.

How can caregivers address possible conflicts within their support groups?

Open communication, active listening, and compassion are essential for addressing conflicts within support groups.

CAREGIVERS BILL OF RIGHTS

The Components of the Caregivers Bill of Rights

The Caregivers Bill of Rights is made up of five components that empower caregivers to take care of themselves while providing care to their loved ones.

These rights include:

• *Right to Self-Care*

Caregivers have a right to take care of their physical and emotional health needs. Taking care of yourself is essential to ensure that you remain healthy and are capable of providing care in the long-term.

• *Right to Seek Assistance*

Taking care of someone with a health issue or disability can be challenging, and caregivers need to have access to resources and support when they need it. This right provides caregivers with the opportunity to seek assistance from family members, medical professionals, and community resources.

• *Right to Balance*

Caregiving can be a full-time job, and it's essential to achieve a balance between your responsibilities as a caregiver and your personal life. This right encourages caregivers to seek out activities that bring them joy and fulfillment outside of caregiving.

• *Right to Respect*

Caregivers have a right to respect from their loved ones and medical professionals. Their opinions and views on the care of their loved ones should be considered when creating care plans.

• *Right to Information*

Caregivers need to have access to information about their loved ones' medical condition and care plan. This right encourages healthcare professionals to provide caregivers with information that will help them provide the best care possible.

How the Caregiver's Bill of Rights Can Improve Caregiving

Implementing the Caregiver's Bill of Rights can improve caregiving in several ways, including:

Improving Overall Health and Well-being

Caregivers who practice self-care and seek assistance when needed are more likely to remain healthy and avoid burnout.

Improved Caregiver-Recipient Relationship

Caregivers who have access to resources and support are better equipped to provide quality care to their loved ones, improving the caregiver-recipient relationship.

Reduced Caregiver Burnout and Stress

Taking care of your physical and emotional health needs can reduce stress and burnout, making caregiving more manageable in the long-term.

The Caregiver's Bill of Rights provides a framework that supports family caregivers and promotes their rights to take care of themselves while caring for their loved ones. These rights can improve care recipients' health outcomes, improve caregiver-recipient relationships, and reduce caregiver stress and burnout.

If you are a caregiver, make sure you familiarize yourself with these rights, and don't be afraid to advocate for your needs. By taking care of yourself, you can provide better care for your loved ones.

A CAREGIVER'S GUIDE TO OVERCOMING

Maximizing the Guide into your Journey

To maximize this guide, we recommend:

- Dedicate regular time to reflect on the information and your experiences.

- Use the guide as a resource for support.

- Connect with support groups or online communities for encouragement.

- Celebrate small victories and acknowledge your growth.

I hope this book has shed light on the emotional challenges faced by full-time caregivers. Over the course of four chapters, we've examined the roots and impacts of frustration, anger, and exhaustion, along with strategies for managing these feelings. I want to underscore the significance of self-care and acknowledge the crucial role caregivers play in our communities.

The insights presented here are designed to empower caregivers to confront their emotional hurdles and prioritize their mental well-being. This guide serves as a resource for cultivating a mindful approach to self-care and building supportive networks, enabling caregivers to enhance their own well-being while caring for their loved ones. My goal is for this guide to contribute to a healthier environment for caregivers.

Remember, overcoming frustration and exhaustion is a gradual process. Be patient with yourself, practice self-compassion, and utilize the resources to enhance your mental health and overall well-being. *Caregivers DO Matter!*

www.**Moore**BooksR.us

OVERCOMING...

A Caregiver's Guide

Explore the emotional struggles and challenges faced by full-time caregivers, delving into the causes, effects, and strategies for overcoming feelings of frustration, anger, stress, guilt and exhaustion. These guides also underscore the vital importance of self-care.

It is essential to acknowledge the immense role that caregivers play in our society, highlighting their personal sacrifices and the profound impact they have on the lives of those they care for. The knowledge shared will serve as a guide for caregivers to embrace a mindful approach to self-care and cultivate supportive communities, fostering improved well-being and enhanced care for their loved ones.

The ultimate goal of this book is to contribute to a healthier, more compassionate society that values the crucial work of caregivers.

Remember, *Caregivers DO Matter.*

OVERCOMING

- Frustration, Anger, & Exhaustion
- Lonliness, Abandonment, & Depression
- Anxiety, Worry, & Stress
- Guilt. Grief, & Regret

www.MooreBooksR.us

Think Feel Speak Write – Do 2.o

A Path Toward Realizing Your Purpose

Many of us are frustrated, confused, and lack enthusiasm; just going through the motions in life. We have settled for the world's definition of who we are instead of agreeing with God who has created us on purpose.

In this book are insights and stories that offer a fresh outlook on how these principles can impact your journey. You too may find that as you Think, Feel, Speak, Write, and DO purposefully, you can live a fulfilling life as God created you to live, with purpose.

Get started today!

www.onecreativemindllc.com/think2 or thinkfeelspeakwritedo2.com

---

"Why Won't They Just Die!"

"Emotional turmoil of Caregivers often goes unnoticed."

When a caregiver experiences the thought, "why won't they just die!" they are not actually expressing a wish for the death of their loved one. It's used in a time when the caregiver feels that they've reached their limit; in a moment of overwhelm, frustration and desperation, where they feel like they're running out of options.

www.whywonttheyjustdie.com

Contact R. Lee Moore, Sr.

For Book Signings &
Speaking Engagements:

RLeeMooreSr@gmail.com

(844) 246-2200

www.RonaldLeeMooreSr.com

R. Lee Moore, Sr.
295 E. Swedesford Road, #288
Wayne, PA 19087

www.**Moore**BooksR.us

www.ingramcontent.com/pod-product-compliance
Lightning Source LLC
Chambersburg PA
CBHW051233120626
46547CB00013B/1625